Character Education

Patience

by Lucia Raatma

Consultant:
Madonna Murphy, Ph.D.
Associate Professor of Education
University of St. Francis, Joliet, Illinois
Author, *Character Education in America's Blue Ribbon Schools*

Bridgestone Books
an imprint of Capstone Press
Mankato, Minnesota

Bridgestone Books are published by Capstone Press
151 Good Counsel Drive, P.O. Box 669, Mankato, Minnesota 56002
http://www.capstone-press.com

Library of Congress Cataloging-in-Publication Data
Raatma, Lucia.
    Patience/by Lucia Raatma.
    p. cm.—(Character education)
    Includes bibliographical references and index.
    Summary: Explains the virtue of patience and how readers can practice it at
home, in the community, and with each other.
    ISBN 0-7368-0508-7
    1. Patience—Juvenile literature. [1. Patience.] I. Title. II. Series.
BJ1533.P3 R23 2000
179'.9—dc21   99-047923

Editorial Credits

Karen L. Daas, editor; Steve Christensen, cover designer; Kimberly Danger,
    photo researcher

Photo Credits

Archive Photos, 18
Frances M. Roberts, 20
International Stock/Elliot Varner Smith, 6
Kim Stanton, cover
Marilyn Moseley LaMantia, 14
Matt Swinden, 4, 16
Photo Network/Myrleen Cate, 8
Unicorn Stock Photos/Martha McBride, 12
Visuals Unlimited, 10

1 2 3 4 5 6 05 04 03 02 01 00

Table of Contents

Patience

Patience means waiting calmly without complaining. You may want to play a game. But you do not know the rules. You can be patient and listen to directions. Patient people understand they cannot always do what they want right away.

Patience with Yourself

Being patient with yourself means giving yourself time to learn new skills. You may want to play a song right away. But you have to practice hard first. Patient people understand they must work hard to reach goals.

goal
something that you plan for
or work toward finishing

Patience with Your Family

Your family members may not always do what you want. You want your mom to take you to the park. But you have to wait until she is not busy. Patient people do not complain while they wait.

Patience with Your Friends

You may want your friends to play a new game with you. But you need to teach them the rules. One friend may not understand the game's rules at first. A patient person explains the rules again.

Patience in Sports

You may be eager to show your skills in a softball game. But it is important to be patient. Wait for your turn at bat. Be patient with your teammates too. They may strike out or drop the ball. Remember that no one is perfect.

Patience at School

School does not always go smoothly. Someone may accidentally knock your books on the floor. A patient person calmly picks up the books. Being patient means calmly dealing with problems.

Patience in Your Community

You can show patience in your community. You may have to wait in line to use the slide at the park. Patient people do not cut in line or push people in front of them. Patient people calmly wait for their turn.

"Truly, civilization is the result of long ages of patient, purposeful teaching."
—Anne Sullivan (right)

Patience and Anne Sullivan

Anne Sullivan was Helen Keller's teacher. Helen was both deaf and blind. She could not learn in the same way other people did. Anne was patient with Helen. She found new ways to teach Helen. She taught Helen how to share ideas using a manual alphabet.

manual alphabet
movements similar to sign language performed into the hands of another person

Patience and You

Patient people know that waiting for rewards is worthwhile. Being patient can help you learn new skills and meet goals. Patience also can help you get along with others. Being patient with others shows that you care for them.

Hands On: Growing Plants

We sometimes want things to happen quickly. But often we have to wait. Being patient often leads to rewards.

What You Need
Planting flat or plastic tray
Potting soil
Packet of seeds
Watering can and water
A sunny place

What You Do
1. Fill the flat with potting soil. Follow the directions on the seed packet. These directions will tell you how far apart and how deep the holes should be.
2. Stick your fingers into the soil to make a few small holes.
3. Put a few seeds in each hole.
4. Cover each hole with soil.
5. Water the seeds until the soil is moist.
6. Place the flat in a sunny place.
7. Keep the soil moist. Follow the watering directions on the seed packet.

Caring for plants and waiting for them to grow shows your patience. You will be rewarded with beautiful flowers or tasty vegetables.

Words to Know

civilization (siv-i-luh-ZAY-shuhn)—an organized community

complain (kuhm-PLAYN)—to say you are unhappy about something

goal (GOHL)—something that you plan for or work toward finishing

manual alphabet (MAN-yoo-uhl AL-fuh-bet)—movements similar to sign language performed into the hands of another person

reward (ri-WAWRD)—something you get for doing something well

▼ Read More

Sullivan, George. *Helen Keller.* In Their Own Words. New York: Scholastic, 2000.
Wagner, Cheryl V. *It's Taking Too Long: A Book About Patience.* The Big Comfy Couch. Alexandria, Va.: Time Life, 1996.
Walters, Catherine. *When Will It Be Spring?* New York: Dutton Children's Books, 1998.

▼ Internet Sites

American Sign Language Fingerspelling
http://where.com/scott.net/asl
Annie Mansfield Sullivan Macy
http://www.afb.org/fs_asm.html
Character Counts! National Home Page
http://www.charactercounts.org

▼ Index